JOURNEYS

JOURNEYS

Kathleen Cain

© Kathleen Cain 2018

All rights reserved. No part of this book may be reproduced or transmitted in any form or by any means, electronic or mechanical or by any information or storage and retrieval system without permission in writing from the author or publisher.

Some of these works have appeared in the following volumes: Columbia Chapter of the Missouri Writers' Guild publication, *Well Versed 2013,* Columbia Art League's *Interpretations IV* 2016, and Creative Writing of Columbia's anthology, *Eternal as a Weed,* 2017 Bridget Bufford, Editor.

Cover Art and Section break illustrations by Kate Gray © All rights reserved

Layout by Yolanda Ciolli

Compass
Flower
Press

Published by Compass Flower Press
Columbia, Missouri

ISBN 978-1-942168-87-4

For Stephen

*"Deep, So deep, the voice of the sea
Calls to me in captivity,
Wondering earth-child set me free,
And one of us you then will be."*

—Vere L. Mathews
Fanta-sea Children

Table of Contents

I   Waking

A Thread 15
Opening 16
Waking 17
Chasing Joy 18
Cacophony 19
Night 20
The Ride 21
Cracked Mirror 22

II   Paper Fences

Bones 27
Yellow Dog 28
Alone 29
Moose 30
Mardi Gras Mask 31
Seeking 32
Rider 34
Mort 35
Anthracite Eyes 37

III   Warm Creek Utah

My Town 41
Where I Come From 42
Snow Leopard 44
What Lingers 46
Warm Creek Utah 47
The Crow 48
Sorrow 49
Regaining Me 50
Fever 51

IV   Rainbow Lake

Letting Go 55
If I could Fly 56
Looking for Light 57
Butterflies 58
Bess 59
Chels 60
For Luna 61
The Room 62
In Case of Fire 64
Rainbow Lake 65

V   Sunday *Times*

Aleppo 69
Darfur Woman 70
November 8 71
Sunday, *New York Times* 72
Bejing 73
Muted Autumn 74
Legacy 75

VI   Snakes Rest

February 79
Panther Dreams 80
Fran 81
Gratitude 82
July 83
October 84
December 85
The Snakes Rest 86
Winter 88

I Waking

A Thread

Morning spider's filament
Spun from her belly

Thoughtless I've passed through them
On early walks
Annoyance

Only to realize later
That threads are binding

The stuff that crosses the path

And makes us whole.

Opening

As though it is just light
The promise of morning
Enters my mind

Pushing the cells in my brain
Accept this

A change about hope

The infusion
After years of absence

Strange, as though I'm in an orchestra
Practicing to a metronome
And the rhythm suddenly changes

Syncopation
Becomes slow
From a polka to a waltz

Waking

Morning light

No longer the excuse of darkness

Sleep slides out the window through the crack I leave open each night.

One morning I follow,
squeezing through the crack
to join her smoky movements

I've known for years I could fly
But it's been long enough
that I have to catch her tail to stay up

It is Spring and I can feel the cool
and the warm that mix in the morning air

We weave through the budding trees, touching some softly
I move up on her tail—holding her tightly with my whole body,
my nightclothes wet with dew.

Should we go too high, I can't return and my fear intrudes,

I hold her even tighter.

She smiles as she turns, gliding me sweetly
back through the crack, then vanishes

I stand at the mirror, wet
Toothbrush in my hand

Chasing Joy

Fat bead of quicksilver
Moves through your fingers
Hits the floor and scatters

You scramble to your knees
Try to retrieve the beads

As though it matters

When you recall the moose
An evening when you expected nothing
But the peace of the mountains

He appeared
His rack majestic
His silhouette absurd

He moved amid the tall scrub
And disappeared

As you breathed in the clear air
And contemplated the real meaning of gratitude.

Cacophony

That last August night in the Rockies
Dark arms seem to embrace you as a lover might
You gaze at the peak's silhouette
Meteors streak silently past.

At dawn you begin the descent
Moving down the winding road
To join the curveless section of interstate
Through the Great Plains
The remarkable beauty of the Flint Hills,
Move into river country.

High bluffs announce the great waterway
As humidity replaces the cool dry of yesterday.

Night again, eight hundred miles east
The cacophony of insect noise invades, crescendos,
Repeats, settles, repeats.

You try to sleep
Wrapped in this lush place
Wondering of the cool silence you left behind.

Night

You let in early night
Right before all light leaves

Nighthawks signal the end as they pass
Along the back wall of your vision
Shrieks follow in their wake as they swoop and dive

Dark floods the sky
Stars, those luminous wonders,
Pop from a place of mystery

You go inside.

Ink invades your soul as you settle
Wait for sleep
Release from all that was this day

A full moon rises
You contemplate hope
In the embrace of silence

Slumber escorts you
To dreams of birds

Folding their wings.

The Ride

He picked me up in his car at about eleven one night. He wore a dark blue wool shirt. His hair cut and combed just so; I could see his profile from the passenger seat. It was strong, almost chiseled. He drove with one hand, the other in his lap.

I'd been in some of the neighborhoods before but this time they were just silhouettes. A few lights were visible in upstairs windows. Porches, front walks, even streetlights were dark.

The dark had a mystical effect on Mark. His smile reflected from the moon outside the car window, which bore in on us, an invasion from that other place where he spent his days.

I asked him if he did this often, these late night drive arounds. He indicated he did. He found a sense of peace when most others were asleep. I was fascinated with his hand on the steering wheel. It had a sexy way of controlling the car, and by association, me. I'd never thought of him that way, but now I was staring. Deeper in my awareness was that his sexiness came from a sinister place, one I'd missed in him when he was alive.

His control of the dark and of my time with him was complete. We did not talk about me, about my day, my life. We just drove while I looked. The blue shirt was perfect, cut just so. His profile remained all that I saw. He may not have had a complete face. It didn't matter.

I don't remember coming home.

Cracked mirror

A slash of lightning
Divides your face
A split mask

Your right eye looks out from goodness
Emanating bird songs in early morning
The music of a harp
Played by a winged angel
Your blue eye
Sitting atop a rosy cheek
Virginal

Your left side, a summer storm
Just gathering along the west horizon
Pulling in early darkness long before sunset
This eye fathomless, unlit.

You smile
A contortion grins back
One side turned up
Perfect lips, pink and dewy
While the other turns down
Lips pulled back to reveal a row of teeth
Sooty from too much use

Tethered to this image, you see too much
An instant flickers past
As your mind takes in this portrait
Soaking you with dread and knowing
You cannot move

You watch as your image begins to swirl
Turn to liquid
Merge
Pink and dark the colors form a stream
In which teeth float like boats on summer runoff
The storm having come and gone

The crack has vanished, the mirror restored
It is empty

You watch in horror
Even as you look
The wall behind the mirror fills with dark streaks
Red and black their sinister trip
Moves down
Soon to join the floor
Meet your bare feet

Your shadow will ascend
The heat beyond bearing

II Paper Fences

Bones

My brother's words come back to me as I pass this place
"Ah, the autumn breeze makes bones of trees
Lacy bones, they mingle with the sky."

They form a pale mobile
Which hangs from a dry tree, dancing in the wind.

Wire joins them
Skin, blood, fat, nerves
All gone.

I pass this skeleton with haste
It taunts my eye
In the far corner of my vision.

Scarecrow of the glade
Delicate tarsals, metatarsals, translucent with age
Windwalk above the ground in early November.

My vision takes in the grin
The deathly gaping smile
Which calls in and stores darkness.

I quicken my pace

Some day
This will be me.

For now, this day
My flesh remains
Covering what I know is within.

Short, bare, cruel November has arrived.

I draw my scarf across my chin.

Yellow Dog

Silent
At my right heel
She follows
Spirit guide
Friend

Her brown soulful eyes
Regard me
Have my back

She trots along
Stops when I stop

One day she will stop for good

And what will I do?

Alone

I see a crepe paper fence
Being made by children

When completed, it will obscure the light.

Leaving the viewer alone
In his last moments

A door's creak summons the closing
A latch clicks

Darkness floods the space

While offspring flourish

On the other side.

Moose

At first a shadow
You only felt
The moose emerged from the aspen
Deep eyes on you.

You backed down the trail
Giving way for him to proceed down the mountain.

A gift, you think
Large prey
Making his way to the wetlands below
Where he will sleep.

And now, another shadow joins you
He walks on your left
Gentle predator.

You breathe in the mountain air
Gratitude on your right
Reminding you of the gift
Of this place and time.

Precious
Fragile

You recall his visit to your friend
It was not gentle
There was little time for gratitude
Before he claimed her.

You wonder at his restraint with you.

Mardi Gras Mask

Tepid water enters your soul
Stills your breath
Forcing your eyes to see the hydras looming
Memories dance across your vision

Once settled into that place
You can see the screen

Mardi Gras masks
Sweet smiling faces
Clowns' grimaces

You sink into this place

This surreal world
That is loss

You watch
Wait

Look for the last act of this play

That is grief

Seeking

A reflection in a pond
Built by trees and sun
Or a cloud formation building before a storm
A shadow, perhaps
Even a dream

Appearing without my bidding
Each has something to say
Wordless
They show themselves
Dissolve
Leave their memory

Now imprinted on my brain
Part of the vast storage
Which, sometimes at my bidding
Returns
Carrying messages

Then, just before the words appear
The clarity I so desire
Again they vanish
To rest, just below my consciousness

I grasp at these faces, these beings without flesh
That other world I know exists
The one that surrounds me
Teases me
Melts

Sometimes I see those I've lost to this region
They surround me as a cloak
That gives off no warmth

I try to grasp it
Hold it up to the light
It dissolves from my touch
Recedes
Waits
Returning only when I forget

Rider

Light leaves the woods as water might
Flowing out
Replaced by long tree shadows
Which seep until they meet and become black.

The horse steps carefully
Reins held deftly by its rider
Head set to the chest
A living team needing no words.

They move
Into the darkness of this realm
Reemerging
As moon shadows

That place, not yet visible
Waits as always
For rider and steed.

Now, dissolving from view
Tree, man and animal
Cast no shadow
Make no sound.

Aided by memory,
They proceed through this night

A meadow lies ahead
Lush with spring green
Where they will lie.

Horse and rider
Cupped as lovers
To wait for the sun.

No trace of their passing will be found.

I recede into the trees
Wait for their next passing
Some moon filled night
I will join them.

Mort

Long ago images penetrate your sleep
Soundless music.

Memories, unedited, stream across your vision
Their energy beyond your control
Disorderly.

You wake exhausted
Set out for another stroll with him.
Today, you lock hands,
His cold.

You see the trees swallowed by deep snow
In the photo on your desk
Another place.

Returned now to this place
You realize the breeze sends the music of autumn
The sounds of dry leaves, ballerinas poised to fall.

You think of the sounds in those mountains
Where trees moan
Prostitutes to the wind.

Anthracite Eyes

Red embers gaze out from rock topped with marl

I walk along an abandoned rail passage
Blasted long ago

To move people and coal

A reminder of the past

Life compressed through eons

Soon to be diamonds

III Warm Creek Utah

My Town

A gossamer tunnel guides my descent
Into memories

The years pass as scenes on a train

Grade school innocence
Brownie Scouts

Dad/Daughter date night

The highway passes through this tunnel
To those who share these memories

Judy, with her glamorous mother
Make up, scarves, mirror at the ready

Janet, raised with brothers, paneled station wagon, and
farting dog.

Gretchen, with her fearsome mother who cooked a sour
cream pie I still crave.

Roxanne of the beautiful house of sisters and little brother
  Craig, now a man
who plays his guitar and sings in this county where we
  grew up.

Carol, cheerleader supreme
Who gave such loving presence
to Judy Pat in her last days.

Where I Come From

I am from Mary Brown's daughters' hand me downs
       starched, white blouses my favorites

Mary Kumm's gift shop
       which she operated despite her mighty leg braces
       the shop never cleaned
       filled with passages

Summers in Mormon primary class in Manti
       where I learned I was a Gentile

St. Peter's Episcopal church
       with the rectory next door
       the romance of Father Minturn's cigarette glowing
         on the Rectory porch

Mrs. Smith's violin lessons in the fall
       walking home to the smell of apples stewing
       sausage and milk gravy ready
       early dark

My father's ashtray beside the winged chair
       Smoke rising above the back of his head

I am from memories
       of my brother reciting lines from *Desire Under the Elms*
         at night
       outside my bedroom window
       his prescient way in our town

       my sister's nocturnal visits to the roof

       my own night time tree branch where I could see
         the lights go out in houses around us
       their softness revealed by the lack of sound

All these memories pile up now
        tumble and shuffle for a place
        dusty boxes with ribbon ties

My morning dreams now pull me back, asleep
        where Mother appears
        talks to me, smiles in her youth

I am from Spring, so many now
        with daffodils, rain, the mighty appearance of hostas
        the knowing of summer droughts
        so impossible to consider
        as the dark, moldy leaves cover the corners of my garden

Mrs. Smith, Father Minturn, Mary Brown, Mary Kumm,
Mother, my father all come and go as they please
    in the place without walls where I am from.

Snow Leopard

You remember the magic of watching the sun
come up behind the mountains east of Manti, Utah.

These mountains full of green pine
and quaking aspen.
You still remember when just before dawn,
you would go out with him,
crouch in anticipation in the cool morning,
try to stay perfectly still, stare with eyes watering
from the effort and wait,
watching the light and then, if you were lucky,
you would see the orb, impossibly bright, pop up.
It was an impossibly sweet time
with this wise, loving man.

Then there were the times
at night when he would build a pile of bread chunks
in two bowls, sprinkle sugar on top
and fill both with cream from the cellar.
The cream all the better,
since stolen, as your grandmother didn't believe
he should have it.

Then, at bedtime, you would think
of the next morning and your pursuit of the sun,
as though it were a new experience.
Rare as the snow leopard,
something only a few people ever get to see
and cherish.

Sometimes he would walk with you,
show you animal tracks,
quiz you on the easy ones,
help you feel wise,
practice for later life.
He taught you phrases in Paiute,
spoken with reverence.

This man, your grandfather,
always had time for you during those visits,
visits that sustained you throughout the year.
And as impossible as it may seem,
these many years past, they still do.

What Lingers

I'd been in the woods for days
A wander I did not plan
Yet there I was

So long ago

A cabin appeared
And I noticed that I was hungry

Inside, a table was set

Porridge, I thought

Greedily, I ate till sated.

The taste remains.

Warm Creek Utah

My six year old me
Recalls this place
Where peace and pleasure mixed
With innocence
So long ago

And yet
Here it is again
A place for the heart to heal

My bare toes mix with the impossibly luscious silt
An infusion of joy and portent
Delicious sadness
I could not begin to understand
Yet knew would come

Watercress abounded
It's crisp taste new then

I stepped out of the springs
My blood
My heart
And indeed my soul
Gathered that moment
Stored it

Till now
When I need it most

I close my eyes
Embrace the child
Breathe out the sorrow
And once again, taste the cress.

The Crow

Estrogen, that winged savior, was poised in the dry tree that no one in the house but she, could see. Mocking in his superior, unreachable guarantee of easing her journey, fixing his gaze on her each morning, a fucking crow bearing down, red eyes piercing her solitude as she contemplated another day.

She can barely recall that last trickling. She enjoyed that time, the release, the menacing power of blood.

"It's the size of a walnut," the doctor said as she eased out of the stirrups and sat up. Her breasts had been liberated years ago due to cancer and now her uterus was a useless nut. She looked at her bare feet, noticing the slight indentation from the stirrups.

Products for dryness sang out merrily from a section of the drug store she'd never noticed but now prowled looking furtive enough to set off shoplifter alarms were anyone watching.

One day, it was simply over, signaling a passage into a place of womanly futility, a pushing aside.

It was then she recalled the photos of her mother, on a cruise, her beauty replaced by a lumpy look, so sudden, it was as though she'd gone into a room, closed the door and had been replaced by someone who embarrassed her daughter. In ten years she returned with such a blast of energy and piercing old age wisdom, it was astonishing. The beautician who had been coloring her hair a dull orange brown was dismissed and the purest white emerged, framing her startling sapphire eyes.

She doesn't like to look at her own photos of that time, the worst of which was at her son's wedding. She wore a sequined top, ghastly in its poor taste.

But now, she's dismissed the crow. He can deal his drugs elsewhere. She's moved on.

Sorrow

A visitor you don't invite
Joins your walk

She stalks your dogs
Waits as you do beside the stream where they stop to drink

A shadow, she has been your companion for a while

Today she precedes you up the last hill

You watch with wonder at her silhouette against the horizon
On tiptoe, she moves her arms skyward

Large wings sprout, blocking out the sunlight

Gently, she lowers them
Waits for you to catch up

She will leave you

Not yet

But soon

Regaining Me

I've sent tentacles out too far it seems
Roots, looking for sun above shallow soil

Regaining youth
Too elusive
Yet seductive

Alas
The roots I ignore are the taps
The ones that know where the water lies

I remember the deep snow of a cold Colorado morning

Tonight I hear owls
Calling in the woods

It is spring
And their purpose is riotous

I take it for granted

As I search for the deep water

Which has been eluding me these days

Hold me, dear Earth.

Fever

Your cool hand touches his brow
Hot with fever.

You stroke his head
Notice his breathing.

You place your hands on his neck
Hoping the fever will warm you
Ground you.

Shallow breath escapes his agape mouth
Pulled down by gravity.

This man,
whose hands have steadied you.

In sleep he looks older.

So many years his hands
Firm around your ankles
Have helped you find the earth
when you might have flown away.

And now,
ask him to stay

You imagine the two of you in some meadow
Your hands joined
Wet faces look to the sky
Smile with gratitude and joy.

IV Rainbow Lake

Letting Go

Perched on your hand
The bird you rescued long ago
Fluffs her feathers

Thin, twig-like claws
Are drawn around your fingers
Not ready, you worry

You want to hold her back
Knowing you might crush those fragile bones
Just to keep her here

Still, you raise your hand gently
Feel the claws loosen
Watch her rise

As she leaves, the space created in your heart
Begins to fill
Dark liquid replaced with hope

A shadow passes high above
Its winged shape reflected below

You rest

If I Could Fly

I would swirl upward
A tiny cyclone
First vertical

Sound below would vanish
As I lay out aligned with the ground
My arms would spread out to become wings
They would grow long, as Gabriel's

I would soar, eagle-like
Astounded at the sudden stillness
The quiet
Noises below now mere murmurs

My eyes would scan the crowd below
for movement
Imagining them as mice

I would feel the air
As air should be felt
A bath of breezes,
a protective cushion from gravity's pull

A place to swim
A womb above the earth

Looking for Light

A paintbrush spreads dark words
Through the clear water
Flowing through my mind

They crowd into the river
Dissolve
Forming a stream of sorrow

A cruel cloak of sadness embraces me
Pulls me along the current

Love, more than I've ever known
Grabs my heart
Taking my breath as dread creeps into my dreams

I wake tired
Face the day after

My senses leave me as I feel the wings of flight
Lifting me above what's real

Don't leave me dear one
Please

Butterflies

A woven silk scarf trails me
Yellow daffodils
Monkey-faced narcissus
Lilac and crocus

Along for the ride
They flutter off in the breezes
As I move along the trail this spring day

I come to a place where the creek widens
And a pool is formed
Wide enough for my canine companions

My scarf
Settles in the stillness
I let my fingers move aimlessly along the silk
Letting the fabric release some of what is still in its folds.

Memories fly out like small butterflies

A slight breeze escapes from the entrapment of the trees
The butterflies move with it
Away, before I can even detect their color
Their beautiful patterns.

I wrap the scarf tight around me
Hold it close
Call my dogs and resume my walk
This time faster
As though I know where I am going

My memories safe.

Bess

(For Nancy)

She believed in sunspots

The fourth dimension

And the liberal use of our middle names

Naturally tight hair
And a wicked smile

She smoked behind the greenhouse
So we couldn't see

Alice's daughter
Utah woman
Transplanted to the plains

I could see the mountains
in her remarkable blue eyes

Chels

I know you through his words
Endearing, proud

I imagine his smile as he speaks with quiet reverence
About the child he raised.
Your journey to woman, wife, and mother.

His pride at all you manage filled with the wonder of it all.
Your beauty, grace under too much burden

But also what he doesn't say but hopes dearly.

That you deserve joy
Not just the call to stay strong
But to be loved and protected
Along life's trek

To be safe
Really safe
And free

To fly and land lightly
In a place of caring.

For Luna

Few know the journey they made
A trek from outside
To a truth deep inside.

Dresses foreign to this little girl
Childhood surrounded
With a language unspoken

As though speaking it could only be safe in the dark.

Together they joined hands
Set out
Found others.

Grew bold
Asked for help.

That trip is almost over.

Married now they smile at the planet they had to wander
Open their arms in welcome to those
Whose journeys have just begun.

The Room

The room is small
You notice its walls seem to move
You've been here too long, you think, the idea of moving walls
Nonsense

And then they move
As they have every day
Years now

The walls
Closer in
How many days, months, years?
You can't remember
You try to make your mind recall
The first time you bought one of those pill containers

You know, the ones with "morning, noon, evening, bedtime"
gaily printed
The ones with the lids for easy loading
So you don't forget when to take what

The ones you do forget
Or the lids come off in your purse
Or bedtime, loading the pills wrong because you are distracted

And then, you are back in the room
That little room with the walls

The walls are pink
You detest pink

You lie down and wait for it to end this day
Perhaps tomorrow will be better

Your friends ask, "Do you think it is the humidity?"
Or, "Is it because.....?"

You answer

It doesn't really matter what you say
The walls move

They are on their own course.

In Case of Fire

The dining hall emptied
As residents returned to their rooms after lunch.

I waited at the elevator
As heads gathered around me

I heard the soft hum of Michael's power chair
As I pondered the sign

It read, "In case of fire, use stairs."

Rainbow Lake

Night, the skirted lady, left an hour ago

I see her passing in the shadows of early morning on new snow
Her dark cloak lingers below the cruel beauty of ice on trees
Filtered with the rising sun

Cold
My nemesis and lover
Feeds my longing for solitude

Beckoning me up this trail
To the frozen lake

Where I am embraced with gratitude
With all it is to be alive.

As I rest, I notice my fingers are warm
Recovered within my gloves
Breath comes easier as I lower my neckpiece

Pole in hand
I descend to begin my day
Dogs preceding me leaving puffs of cold air
To mark my way.

V Sunday *Times*

Aleppo

Airplanes pass high above
Leaving shadows in their wake
As lethal cargo
Violates the sanctity of places of healing

Syria

Condemned by
Blood stained crossed timbers

They lie askew
On hope's white ashes

Caduceus emerges without wings
Its skeletal shape, fragile, incomplete

There is no safe place here

Time is short
Before full darkness descends

And no sound can escape.

Phoenix lurks

Darfur Woman

You bring a presence
     It startles most

You sit in stillness
     Your mouth a closed door
     Your eyes vacant
     For what they have seen cannot be held
     The reduction of things to dust.

You have no cup, no bowl, not even a glass

Meanwhile we worry about our things
     We sort and fret
     Not knowing how little they matter
     How quickly they can vanish

You disturb us with your vacant hole of knowing

I look at my shadow
     Notice my ghost

I go back to my things
     While you sit and breathe

A Buddha among us.

November 8

There is an elephant on my chest

Big ass
Swinging trunk

Nothing like the creature in the wild
This one spends time in china shops
Digs up my backyard
Endangers those I love

Size
Dominance
Bestows power
To reign as tho King

Once he eats all that is in sight
Stomps the ground into dust
Consumes all the water

He will lift his great proboscis to the sky
And yell for help

I will be far away
Building Eden in some other place

To which he cannot travel
As I will have ripped up all the rails and roads
And retreated to somewhere green and safe.

Sunday, *New York Times*

Stories in which kindness recedes
      To dark stone in their eyes
      Pupils no longer able to let in light

They raped, murdered and burned children
Annihilation fueled by blind hate

Some survived
Victims with babies in their bellies

While cold ashes pile up
Kindness sleeps the sleep of the dead

In another story
      Visitors embark from the large official airplane
      To view the recent floods on an island

The lady's stilettos pick their way, unsullied
Across the ruins.

Beijing

From my window I see her willows
Struggling to breathe

I think of home
Where prairie grass grows over depleted aquifers
And souls are sapped with desert wind.

This generation
Born to hope
Faces the Tsunami of greed

And exits
Too often barren.

Muted Autumn

September dried the leaves
Creating dust
Thick enough to cover the path

My world had turned to black and white
Joy replaced with the quiet breathing
Of one hiding

Until things change

And the explosion of colors
Are once again, safe.

Legacy

I enter a room
Airless
Its soul withdrawn in sinister heat

Men don uniforms for the day
And set out to load another ship

I watch in horror
As one by one
The naked and chained
Receive their brands

Men whose rage is quiet, civilized
Passed down to today's ancestors

Shamed by the beauty and strength
Of those branded ancestors

Whose voices and songs soar to the heavens
Bodies glisten with beauty
As they dance

Offer ideas with humble elegance

Some take a knee

VI Snakes Rest

February

Colors retreat as the earth sleeps
Cracks form in dry cold land
Giving rise to wraith-like shapes
Which loosely surround me

I wonder at their mystery
As they escort me on my walk

Familiar, I think
Yet so cold.

Panther Dreams

The ring-tailed cat grew large
      Another joined.

Together they moved in the tall winter-bare trees
      Above the house where I lay sleeping,

Powerful shadows in leafless trees.

Portent in the cold March night.

Fran

Coiled inside the basket that is her heart
A cobra waits
Her head unfurls up to scan her surroundings
Lazily taking stock of those she loves.

An innocent toddler
A daughter filled with the days of motherhood
Others, not in her vision
But cached in her sphere.

Her head moves languidly, side to side
Tongue flicks, seeking
She recedes to her basket.

Then, one day as she scanned
A woman fell
Just outside her door.

The basket discarded
She moved
Dangerous instinct fueled by love

She did what had to be done
Body lengthened sleek with purpose.

Soon she will retreat to the basket
Coiled and ready for what's next.

Gratitude

Sunlight licks the air
Sending beams through winter weary windows
Leafless trees offer little resistance

Hopeful shadows grace my wood floor
Sending sweet welcome to my depleted soul
On this rare cloudless early April day

July

July's cloak descends on me
Closing in humidity

Stillness abounds
Pierced only by the sounds of the cicadas
Low hums rise to crescendos
Subside, repeat

I ascend into the trees
On stairs formed by roots

Along the cliff yellow dots of leaves appear
Reminiscent of the power of seasons
Deep in the psyche

An ice storm builds in deep winter
Where animals and seeds sleep.

October

October just arrived
The corn has tassled and turned brown
The long heat has vanished
Replaced by welcome cool

It's been hot too long this season
The foliage and I are both dry

I will take pleasure as
Halloween's orange and red costumes trail off
In the breezes that precede November

Revealing silhouettes

I welcome those barren shapes
Against a pale blue sky

Migrating birds pass above
Peace descends as cold moves in

Awaiting the first snowfall
When white crystals will drift soundlessly onto branches

The world returns to shades of gray.

December

       You cross the creek
The park is empty
Last night's rains now pooled water
On saturated ground

The path through the woods
Moves
Making its way, snakelike, down to the swollen creek
Flowing below the bluffs

Deep into the wood traffic sounds grow dim
As water takes over
Churning brown and menacing
You see it below
Hear its force.

As you traverse the ridge
He appears
How long has he been with you?
You can't say

"Are you limping?" he whispers
"A bit," I reply. "Probably the damp."
"Arthritis," he comments.
"Natural, as you age."

Is that a smile, or a leer?

"Not now," he whispers.
"But I won't wait forever, you know."
A bony finger scolds, as he backs into the undergrowth
Disappears.

White sycamores rise
Above dark timber
Winter's bones.

More rain is forecast.

Snakes Rest

I'm walking in the woods
My dogs, their delight so predictable
Joy, I think

My eyes drift soundlessly across the path
Up to the leaves, drooping
In a soft rain
Muted light intensifies the blood orange of a perfect leaf

Oak, pointed pattern repeated in the millions
Each one impeccable in design
Falling with its own internal rhythm
Delighting my eyes
Adorning the path
As it becomes a carpet of fall

I notice the black
Logs, water soaked
They punctuate the color riot
Remind me of the winter that is to come

Squirrels scamper, interrupting the silence
Commuters at the end of the day

And then, as though at some unknown cue
Birds, at first just one, then more

An orchestra is tuning up
Tiny sounds, all dropping like snowflakes
They build to an exquisite crescendo
As I pop out of the woods
To the common path

The dogs wait for their leashes
I snap them on
We move across the bridge
To my car
Traffic
The road home
Reentry

My memories refreshed
The woods quietly settle
To early dark
The birds fold into sleep

Squirrels bury their harvest

The snakes were asleep hours ago.

Winter

December days are short
A time of reflection
Perhaps even dread
As nights descend early

Winters stack one upon another
Accordions
Acquiring dust and portent

We say goodbye to those who leave
Contemplate our own passing
But only on the surface
Like spiders skimming a pond in early spring

A wind passed through last night
Strewing small branches on the path where I walk

I delight in my dog's pursuit of squirrels
Until I think of her success
A limp body in her jaws

Brutal, precious, delicious life

My aloneness startles me.

www.ingramcontent.com/pod-product-compliance
Lightning Source LLC
Chambersburg PA
CBHW020214090426
42734CB00008B/1059